The Lay

Consisting Of Poems Occasioned By The Recent Visit Of Lafayette To The United States

Daniel Bryan

Alpha Editions

This edition published in 2021

ISBN : 9789354540288

Design and Setting By
Alpha Editions
www.alphaedis.com
Email - info@alphaedis.com

THE GREETING.

ADVERTISEMENT.

The reader is requested to bear in mind that the following Poem appears in the character of an Address to General Lafayette, in the presence of an immense assembly convened on the plains of Yorktown, to celebrate the anniversary of the surrender at that place to General Washington and his patriotic band, of the British Army under Lord Cornwallis;—that this glorious event formed the closing scene of the American Revolution—and that General Lafayette there met, after an absence of forty years, a remnant of those gallant veterans who had partaken with him the dangers and the triumphs of that ever-memorable day.

The author would here take occasion to disclaim the indulgence of any illiberal sentiments towards the British nation. In the strong language which he uses in adverting to the oppressive measures exercised by the British Government against her American colonies, he wishes to be distinctly understood as intending only to characterise as tyrannical, the exceptionable acts themselves, and the administration by which they were adopted. For the great body of the English nation, whom he knows to be humane, virtuous, and enlightened, he feels the highest respect; and, while he regards as immeasurably preferable the free republican institutions of his own country, he sees much in the constitution of the British government to admire; and would be very sorry to suspect that, while professing to be a republican himself, he should be so much under the influence of political bigotry and contracted principles, as to entertain prejudices against the citizens of another country on account of their attachment to the land of their nativity, and of their preference for the government under which they were educated and to which their allegiance is due.

Alexandria, D. C. March 18, 1826.

THE GREETING.

A

POETICAL ADDRESS

SUPPOSED TO HAVE BEEN RECITED

TO

GENERAL LAFAYETTE

AT

Yorktown,

On the 19th October, 1824.

I.

IN the name of our country, great Hero! we come
  To welcome thee here on this day of thy glory;
And we hail thee with music of cannon and drum,
  On these plains once with battle disfigured and gory;
Where the flame of thy sword, and the flash of thy eye,
  Victory's path through the clouds of the conflict illumed,
When Liberty's banner, displayed in the sky,
  Proclaimed that her foe to discomfit was doomed.

II.

Thy presence, like that of some guest from above
  Descended to minister blessings on earth,
Enkindles the fervours of reverence and love
  Wherever the patriot emotions have birth ;
But, *here,* on this glorious arena of Fame,
  Too feeble is language—our voices too faint—
The transports that gush through our breasts to proclaim ;
  No muse can depict them—no pencil can paint.—

III.

When the tempest of Tyranny hung on our shore,
  And the peals of its vengeance our continent shook ;
When the white robes of Freedom were dripping with gore,
  And she drooped as though Hope had her bosom forsook—
Thy gallant young heart, with an ardour divine,
  A devotion as pure as e'er hallowed the soul,
Vowed to yield the last throb of its pulse at her shrine,
  Or see her the standard of triumph unrol.—

IV.

Columbia! behold here the champion whose vow,
Thus solemnly made, on this spot was fulfilled!
Here, a branch of that laurel still green on his brow
He plucked, where the blood of the foeman was spilled.
No bankrupt in character, fortune, or friends—
No ambitious, or venal, adventurer was he;
No pang of affliction the heart strings that rends,
Forced him o'er the wide billows for solace to flee.

V.

With the golden dominion of wealth at command,
And arrayed in the honours of title and birth;
In the ecstatic endearments of wedlock's sweet band
United with loveliness, beauty, and worth;
A favourite of Gallia's magnificent court,
And entwined with his infancy's tenderest ties,
He heard, with a bosom all flame, the report
Of the ravaging storm that enveloped our skies.

VI.

As though by a spirit prophetic inspired,
His soul made a flight through the orbit of Time,
In the vast of the future her pinions, untired,
She expanded, contemplating visions sublime:
The prospects effulgent that burst on her eye,
An Elysium of glory and freedom evolved,
Harmonious and grand as the systems on high,
Nor destined to vanish 'till these are dissolved!

VII.

But the country which thus to his Fancy's rapt view
In the luminous flow of pure happiness shone,
Had her mountains and valleys in blood to imbrue,
And grapple in war with the hosts of a throne!
Ere those scenes of delight could around her unfold;
But the vantage in armament, numbers, and skill,
Her opponent combined with the allurements of gold,
Gave him means at discretion to ravage and kill.

VIII.

Inexperienced and young—her resources but few—
  Like Israel's brave youth with the giant of Gath—
Her cause on its justice and Heaven she threw,
  And unshrinkingly met her antagonist's wrath—
With an ardour that none but the generous can feel,
  And a purpose too pure for the selfish to know,
As the contest its terrors began to reveal
  Lafayette proclaimed himself Tyranny's foe!

IX.

From his temples their peace-woven chaplets he tore,
  And consigned the loved tokens to beauty's soft hand;
He cast from his limbs the rich vestments they wore,
  And, transformed as if touched by a magical wand,
The courtly young noble, in armour arrayed,
  The glittering pageants of Monarchy spurned,
And to wield for Columbia his virginal blade
  His magnanimous spirit impatiently burned.—

X.

By duty's all-powerful impetus driven,
From the arms of connubial affection he breaks,
And the golden-linked bondage of Friendship is riven,
As the shores of his dear native France he forsakes.—
Behold! a new world the young Hero receives!
He treads in a region wild, lovely, and free,
Where Nature 'mid fragrance and song interweaves
Her forests of bloom into flowers of glee.—

XI.

"And this," he exclaims, "is the country whose charms,
A tyrant's rude fetter would mangle and mar!
Where the war-demon howls forth his chilling alarms,
And the death-vulture hangs o'er his slaughtering car!
Columbia! a pilgrim approaches thy shrine,
The offerings he brings are his sword and his blood!
O! make him thy champion—his life shall be thine!
He seeks this high honour o'er Ocean's dark flood."

XII.

Lo! the beautiful wood-nymph of Freedom appears!
  Wreaths of blooming magnolia her forehead intwine,
Around her an evergreen mantle she wears,
  And her eyes with effusions of tenderness shine:
Majestic and mild, the young Hero she meets,
  And accepts his devotion with smiles of delight;
His heart to her wishes responsively beats,
  And she points where her votaries sustain the dread fight.

XIII.

Entranced by her blessing and holy embrace,
  His soul is uplifted on pinions of flame,
And, as flies the swift steed in the emulous race,
  He rushes to battle, to conquest, and fame.—
Where danger and carnage bestride the red plain,
  And Death's giant arm, through the dark thundering clouds,
Drives his broad lance and piles up his mountains of slain,
  The whirlwind of conflict our Hero enshrouds!

XIV.

As in the Homerian battles of Troy
  A Deity's presence enkindles new zeal,
So his, through our armies breathed transport and joy,
  Gave might to their sinews, and sharpened their steel.
As his bosom companion, adviser, and friend,
  By the side of our country's great Father he shone,
Sought his own with that Chieftain's high virtues to blend,
  And was lov'd and distinguished as Washington's son!

XV.

The ray of his hopes no reverses could dim,
  No hardship could wither the strength of his arm;
The perils of war had no terrors for him,
  And his soul into crime no seduction could charm.
This soldier of Freedom did more than e'er Cæsar could do,
  He vanquished the Passions, whose terrible breath
Has slaughtered more men than the sword ever slew,
  And form in themselves the great armies of Death.

XVI.

As, careering along his high orbit, the sun—
  In beauty, effulgence, and grandeur arrayed—
Through winter's bleak tempests continues to run,
  Till serene in the heavens his glory's displayed,
And his trophies of conquest unfold their rich blooms;
  Thus sublimely, our Hero, through Freedom's dark war,
Pursues his bright course until, scattering the glooms,
  He beams forth in triumph her joy-kindling star!

XVII.

'Twas *here*, on this ground by our country revered,
  That the angel of victory disclosed to his eye,
The political orbs* which in splendour appeared
  Where now we behold them in Liberty's sky:—
'Twas here, through his counsel and valour combined,
  The crest of Cornwallis was shorn of its plumes,
And the fetters for Freedom's brave patriots designed,
  Were rent and interred in his myrmidons' tombs.

* The American States.

XVIII.

In those moments of transport and deathless renown,
 When the head of the Hydra Oppression was crushed,
When Britannia surrendered the pride of the crown,
 And her Monarch turned pale and her Senators blushed—
How sublime were thy feelings, great champion of right!
 How mature, too, the honours that bloomed round thy youth!
How danced through thy mind in pure visions of light,
 The prospective advances of Virtue and Truth!

XIX.

Let tyrants, whose titles to reverence and fame
 Are recorded on features of anguish and wo—
In the traces of bloodshed, of ruin, and flame—
 In hearts that are broken—and tears that still flow—
Regale on the flatteries of courtiers and slaves,
 And grow drunk with the shoutings of bipeds in chains;
When they vanish no mourner shall weep o'er their graves—
 And no dirge to their manes shall pour its sad strains.

XX.

While the curses of millions their memories brand,
And empires shall shudder and blench at their names;
Thy glory, august as our mountains, will stand,
And brilliant and pure as empyreal flames:
On its heaven-crowned pillars the muses enthroned,
Through cycles of ages thy praise shall resound;
And thy virtues, by none but oppressors disowned,
There inscribed, shall enlighten the nations around.

XXI.

Thy triumphs exalt and ennoble the soul—
They exhibit no trophies of countries laid waste,
No banners ensanguined with murder unrol;
In their garlands of laurel no serpents are traced—
The homage that greets thee in Freedom's domain,
Gushes warm and spontaneous from fountains of joy;
And no sigh wrung by tyranny from bosoms of pain,
Its flow of harmonious delight can annoy.

XXII.

The deeds that have rendered immortal thy name,
In accordance with Heaven's munificent plan,
Have made it their lofty unchangeable aim
To augment and to nurture the comforts of man:
Hence, great patriot of nations! thy country's wide earth!
Thou art loved by the virtuous of every clime—
But *here*, to *this* land, most endeared is thy worth—
For it shares most the proofs of thy goodness sublime.

XXIII.

Hence, with bosoms o'erflowing with reverence and love,
From our hills and our vales, from our villas and towns,
With the rush of a flood, to salute thee, we move;
And with offerings more dear than the homage of crowns,
With the incense of Freedom's pure gratitude, greet thee,
Exhaled from the altars divine of the heart:
And, O! 'tis our prayer that again we may meet thee
In regions of happiness never to part!—

XXIV.

Brave sons of Virginia! strong, strong, is the claim
  That binds your affections to Liberty's friend,
Who, when dangers assailed you, with cheerfulness came,
  Your infancy, parents, and homes, to defend;
The pleasures and luxuries of peace and of wealth,
  With gallant devotion to virtue and right,
He resigned, and, exposing life, fortune, and health,
  Toiled for you by day, and watched round you by night.

XXV.

The sleep of our mothers in safety to guard,
  The bosom of love, and warm couches of down,
He relinquished, for lodgings, cold, shelterless, hard,
  While, serene and unmoved by adversity's frown,
He taught the poor soldier to smile as he bled!
  To think of his country, as, fainting and chill,
His limbs were unclothed, and he hungered for bread,
  And for her the last drop of his life-blood to spill!

XXVI.

What transports of hallowed remembrance awake
  In the meeting this day of companions in war!
Who come in our festal delights to partake,
  All honoured with age, and with many a scar.—
In the concourse around thee so eagerly pressing,
  Lafayette! thou behold'st here and there a white head,
And a time withered hand in pursuit of thy blessing—
  Thou meet'st them as brothers returned from the dead!

XXVII.

Hoary veterans! how kindle and glow through your veins
  The chivalrous fire in your bosoms inurned,
As again ye behold these illustrious plains,
  Where once in victorious battle it burned!
To your fancies' rapt vision the scene re-appears,
  And army meets army in awful array;
Lo! the boasting invader his battlements rears,
  And his engines of slaughter their terrors display.—

XXVIII.

The phalanx of Freedom, judicious and brave,
  Prepare the proud foe in his bulwarks to seize,
To compel his surrender, or make *them* his grave:
  The tempest is lowering! though "still as the breeze"—
It thickens! it darkens!—The war-god is there!
  Hark! 'tis the blast of his trump—'tis the roll of his drums—
That thunders his voice—and that blaze in the air
  Is his lightning—the streams of his rockets and bombs.

XXIX.

Great Washington breathes his high soul through his host,
  Lafayette seems clothed with the spirit of Mars—
Each chieftain maintains like a Spartan his post,
  And would die for his banner of eagle and stars.
The command has gone forth—"The intrenchments assault!"
  Against them the storm in its violence beats—
The cannon-peals roll through the welkin's deep vault,
  And the conflict's enveloped in sulphurous sheets.

XXX.

The ramparts are yielding! and foeman meets foe,
There swords fall on sword-arms, and bayonets drink blood;
Here chieftains are bleeding and soldiers lie low—
But behold where yon warriors, like waves in a flood,
Commingle in all the fierce vengeance of fight—
What hero so gallantly bears through the tide,
And leaves in his wake such a glorious light—
Like a war-ship that proudly in battle doth ride?

XXXI.

He is Freedom's young champion, fair Gallia's brave son,
And now in the enemy's fortress he towers!—
The battle is o'er! and the victory is won—
And the lordly Cornwallis to Washington cowers!—
From lowland to highland—through mountain and dell—
Acclamations of triumph and rapture resound,
And pæans supernal the songs of the jubilee swell,
Where the martyrs of Freedom in glory are crowned.—

XXXII.

Hark! how roll their great names through the chorus divine,
Where are heard in their sweetest and loftiest tones,
The harps of the heavenly minstrels who shine
In the splendour of highest angelical thrones!
And the names, and the deeds, of the mighty who live
In the smiles of the land they have honoured and saved,
Their meed of renown the celestial melodies give,
And Lafayette's on glory's wide arch is engraved.

XXXIII.

Descending through ether on pinions of snow,
The Angel of Peace to our country returns,
Stripes the concave of blue with the dies of her bow,
And enshrines here in separate and beautiful urns,
The dust of the warriors who fell on our plains—
Each nation's apart—yet in nearness arranged—
And her olive tree planting to shade the *remains*—
Bids it flourish and bloom there through ages unchanged.

XXXIV.

She waves her white flag and two figures advance—
  The elder 's a matron commanding and proud in her port—
But she meets with confusion the maiden's sweet glance,
  And her cheek seems of varied passions the sport:—
Her head wears a crown—but its splendour is dim—
  For its richest and loveliest jewel is gone!
On her arm hangs a banner whose emblem, so grim,
  And so couchant, was lately the pride of a throne.—

XXXV.

But now her bold lion is humbled and torn—
  And where laurel and sea-weed once formed his proud lair,
He is stretched on a bed that 's dismantled and torn,
  And his eye is despoiled of its conquering glare.
The younger—though stately—is modest of mien,
  And we know by her costume and aspect benign,
That in her loved presence before we have been,
  And that she is Liberty's guardian divine!

XXXVI.

In her fair hand a wide-waving standard she rears
  On which soars an eagle with eye towards the sun,
And, encircled with clusters of glittering spheres,
  He bears the green trophies in battle-fields won.
* * * * * * * * * *
  * * * * * * * * * *
* * * * * * * * * *
  * * * * * * * * * *

XXXVII.

O'er the dust of their heroes the Goddesses stand!
  Britannia, though sorrowing, wears a stern brow,
And her sighs are controlled by a stoic command;
  But Columbia her head on her bosom doth bow,
While her tremulous hands towards the Heavens she spreads,
  And, imbruing with tears the pure snows of her breast,
O'er the slumbering relics her blessings she sheds,
  And implores that in peace her dear country may rest.

XXXVIII.

The moment is kind to the views of their friend—
The angelic promoter of concord and love—
They are touched by her zeal, and their heart-burnings end,
While in accents as soft as the notes of the dove—
She persuades them in amity's flowery bands
Again to unite—when, behold, they embrace!
And social relations between kindred lands
The stains of unnatural warfare efface.—

XXXIX.

Having burst from Oppression's encumbering thrall,
A prosperous Republic our country becomes,
And as long as a mountain shall rear its huge wall,
And man to the storms of the Ocean succumbs;
While the advances of virtue and science combined,
The blessings that wait upon Freedom display,
And its boundless resources reveal to the mind,
Her sons will ne'er bend to a conqueror's sway.—

XL.

Gallant soldier of Freedom! while here we survey,
  With this remnant of veterans who shared in thy toils,
The happy results of that perilous day
  When the vaunting marauder relinquish'd his spoils;
We behold in thy features the flittings of gloom,
  Which pass like successions of rack o'er the sky:
They tell that thy thoughts then are down in the tomb,
  Where the hallowed remains of our Washington lie:—

XLI.

That loved faces, endeared by the tenderest scenes,
  By moments of danger, of anguish, and death,
From thy view the dark veil of eternity screens;
  That patriots, whom, called by the bugle's shrill breath,
Thou hast seen with impetuous vehemence rushing,
  Where Slaughter's huge scythe was destructively weeping,
And the life-blood of thousands in torrents was gushing—
  Now low in the grave's gloomy chambers are sleeping!

XLII.

But, oh! let us not at their absence repine—
For their slumbers profound are deliciously sweet;
Their heads on their country's dear bosom recline,
And hosannas of Freedom their praises repeat:
And may we not cherish the exquisite hope,
That, disbanding from service these bodies of clay,
We shall soar to the zenith of Heaven's high cope—
And explore with our fathers the planets of day!

XLIII.

Is it not, noble chieftain, thy soul's dearest thought,
That the veterans of Freedom who bled at thy side,
Shall be happy and free where no battles are fought—
And that thou shalt be with them, and with them abide,
Partaking for ever their freedom and bliss—
Where the venom of Tyranny's fang is unknown;
Where his serpents at virtues like thine can ne'er hiss—
And no dungeons can echo with misery's groan!

XLIV.

Is it Fancy's creation that kindles this glow,
Which catches from bosom to bosom around?
That rolls back the blood with such hurried flow,
And causes the heart thus to flutter and bound!—
The moment is solemn! the silence is deep!
The spirits of Heroes from Heaven descend!
They come not with the death-angel's terrible sweep,
But unheard, and unseen!—With our spirits they blend.

XLV.

Their breath is benevolence—their mission benign—
Lafayette, and Freedom, and this sacred Day,
Bring them hither, all holy, from regions divine,
Where odours celestial eternally play.—
These are themes to Religion and Heaven endeared—
For this land is the Temple of Virtue—of God!
Here His creatures are loved—here his precepts revered—
And His power is not mocked by proud Tyranny's nod!

XLVI.

Beatified Fathers! your zeal is not lost—
  Your example through life—your dying behests—
The boon that you left us—the blood that it cost—
  All, all, are remembered—sink deep in our breasts—
Whilst we've arms that can strike, and our bosoms can feel,
  Should the squadrons of despots ere blacken our seas—
Our country's free shores shall be pointed with steel—
  And we'll battle for Freedom in blood to our knees!

XLVII.

To your holy protection, blest shades! we commend
  This reverend warrior—this statesman and sage—
Your early associate and Liberty's friend—
  Oh! give him elysian delights in his age!
No longer let breakers and tempests impede
  The flow of his virtues:—through sunshine and flowers
The course of his life's evening pilgrimage lead—
  Till it ends in Eternity's Heavenly bowers!

XLVIII.

Great apostle of Freedom! though brilliant the beam
 Which plays on our hearts in this moment of joy—
Yet a cloud dims the light of the beautiful stream—
 And its shade for a time must our transports annoy.
Soon, too soon, we must part! and the eyes that now gaze
 On thy venerable form with ecstatic delight,
Will behold thee no more! and the grandeur and blaze
 Of our greetings will vanish, with thee, from our sight.

XLIX.

This mighty assemblage must break and diverge,
 And thousands here met on this consecrate ground,
Shall ne'er meet again till their bodies emerge
 From the darkness that reigns in the grave's narrow bound.
But—all brethren—they live in the land they love best—
 Under laws and a government, too, of their own—
Yes, Lafayette! in thy beloved land of the West—
 Unsoiled by the reptiles that crawl round a throne!

L.

If thou from thy less favoured France could'st return—
And dwell here with spirits congenial to thine—
What new—what ineffable—raptures would burn,
In bosoms that distance no more could disjoin!
To know that with thee we inhaled the same air—
That with thine, too, our footsteps impressed the same land—
And that, henceforth, thy life should our happiness share,
Would yield us more pleasure than monarchs command.

LI.

In behalf of thy darling Columbia we plead,
That when to thy vision the scenes of mortality close,
And thy soul from its bonds of probation is freed,
On her bosom thy mantle may fall and repose!—
As pilgrims their sanctified relics adore,
So the holy deposit our hearts would revere—
And the lovers of Freedom from every shore,
Would bedew and embalm it with many a tear.

LII.

But, oh! there are feelings we would not invade—
  Pardon our zeal, most exalted, most sensitive mind!
Our ardent, our anxious petition we've made—
  Its issue to thee—and our God—is consigned.—
We must part! for a season, at least, we must part—
  But, where'er from our country thy destiny lead—
O, remember! the pulse of a Nation's great heart
  For thy welfare will throb—for thy welfare would bleed!

THE VALEDICTORY.

THE VALEDICTORY.

A

POEM,

IN TWO CANTOS.

Comprising Sketches of the Address of President Adams to General Lafayette, and the General's Reply.

CANTO I.

I.

ON many a sleepless eye the morning rose
  That ushered in the eventful day,
Which witnessed, ere its melancholy close,
  From Freedom's shores her Champion borne away:
A mournful strain upon the early breeze,
  In unison with aching hearts, was poured;
And prayers from hoary men on bended knees,
  From suppliant youth, and prostrate beauty soared—
For blessings on the great and virtuous man,
Ere yet the sun his radiant course began.—

II.

Potomac's kindred cities (1.) roused at dawn,
With honours due to grace the parting scene,
And ere the illustrious warrior had withdrawn,
Once more behold his venerated mien.—
Along their streets no sounds of mirth were heard,
The pomp of solemn grief alone was there;
Its influence breathed in every look and word,
And brought to many an eye the trembling tear:
The gathering crowd proclaims the day's advance,
And blending sighs the painful glooms enhance.

III.

To swell the tide the country pours its waves,
Lo! tender woman comes, and feeble age,
Gray-headed veterans tottering o'er their graves,
The rich, the poor, the peasant, and the sage—
All come to take one lingering, parting view
Of Freedom's favourite—virtue's noblest friend!
To tender him a sad, a long adieu,
And for his weal their prayers in concert blend:
Spontaneous homage theirs of glowing souls,
Whose free-born power no tyrant will controls!

IV.

But who, of all this anxious mingling throng,
Before him shall the nation's proxy stand?
To whom the high momentous task belong
To speak to him the feelings of the land?
Who can so well give utterance to her grief,
Who personate Columbia's self so well,
As her PRESIDING SON—her CIVIC CHIEF?
He feels her anguish, and her love can tell:—
With tenderest ardour beaming from his eyes,
Amid the silent crowd, behold him rise!—

V.

His hand a moment on his heart is pressed
To calm the deep emotions labouring there,
And now, to Freedom's reverend chief addressed,
His soul is poured in accents sweet and clear.
Bright samples of his thoughts the Muse would give,
But how can she their glowing charms portray?
Where find for them those tints that ever live,
And all the force of eloquence display?
Her powers though feeble, and her language faint,
She thus essays his ardent thoughts to paint.

VI.

"Not mine, to-day, exalted chief! the joy,
Which, in thy glorious triumph's bright career,
Has yielded many a rapturous tongue employ
When called to greet thee with their country's cheer;
To me the mournful duty now pertains,
Of tendering you the nation's sad farewell !"—
Here grief a moment drowned the speaker's strains,
While every bosom heaved with deepening swell:
Each tongue exclaimed—"And must—O must we part !"
While anguish burst in sobs from every heart.—

VII.

"No cause obtains"—the orator resumed—
"That we should here minutely trace each deed
That in thy early wreaths of glory bloomed—
They shine around, and "*he that runs may read.*"
Deep-founded as the base of Freedom's dome,
And round its vast magnific pillars twined,
Thy fame, outvying that of Greece or Rome,
Shall flourish here perennial as the mind!
Shall splendours here unfold through every age,
Sublime as e'er adorned the classic page.

VIII.

When Pleasure's brightest lures around thee pressed,
And wealth, and youth, and titled rank, conspired
To yield their potent charms augmented zest,
A holier cause thy generous bosom fired—
The cause of Freedom in a foreign land!
For this, from courtly pomp, and home's loved charms,
From scenes entwined by childhood's flowery band,
And from a blooming wife's enrapturing arms!
Thy spirit bore thee, ere thy manhood's prime,
To aid our fathers in this distant clime.

IX.

No wild delusive hopes—no sordid aim—
Thy gallant, calm, reflecting soul, impelled;
Its patient zeal was fed by virtue's flame,
Which through conflicting storms her powers upheld—
That flame no glooms e'er damped, no perils quenched:
When Death's dark banner waved o'er fields of blood,
And veteran hosts before his vengeance blenched,
Its radiance streamed along the battle flood,
And, lighting thee to victory's honoured goal,
Consigned thy name to glory's deathless roll.

X.

" And now, since years on years have passed away,
And man—in childhood then—is white with time;
The deeds that crowned with fame thy early day,
For loftiest wisdom are not less sublime,
Than for the grandeur of their generous zeal:
The joyful plaudits of a nation's voice
Proclaim the gratitude that millions feel,
For that, thy almost more than human choice,
Which turned the scale of thy exalted mind,
Against such weight, in favour of mankind.

XI.

" When Freedom's battles here were fought and won,
And laurels hung upon thy conquering brow,
Thy work of glory had but just begun,
For thou wert still fair Gallia's faithful son!
From this thy honoured and adopted land,
By thine and our brave Fathers' valour freed,
Thou didst return at duty's high command,
To honour France with many a noble deed;
And, in the sternest ordeal, there to test,
The virtues that inspired thy patriot breast.—

XII.

" While years on years in long succession rolled,
There, through capricious Fortune's frowns and smiles,
Through scenes that made the bravest blood run cold;
In triumph's hour, exposed to courtly wiles,
In all the eventful scenes of war and death,
When Revolution's wildest rage prevailed,
And swept the land with flames and whirlwind breath;
Thy towering soul, with strength that never failed,
Soared on her heaven-ward way thro' sun and cloud,
Nor once from its high course her pinion bowed.

XIII.

" Whilst thou, with all a martyr's sleepless zeal,
Throughout that long career of changeful time,
Wert nobly struggling for thy country's weal;
A favouring auspice ruled Columbia's clime:
Her sons, with whom, in Danger's bloodiest hour,
Thy prayers, thy fortunes, and thy life were joined
To break the shackles of tyrannic power,
And pour the light of Freedom o'er the mind!
Were reaping here the harvests of thy toil,
And planting Freedom's fruits in Freedom's soil.

XIV.

Comporting with its more than golden cost,
A nation here, of happiest structure, rose,
Whose spreading bounds, in mighty distance lost,
A vast asylum form for human woes;—
Whose strength, increasing with increasing age,
Not all th' imperial hosts of earth can shake;
Whose worth shall stand approved on History's page
While virtue's self can virtuous feelings wake;
Whose lofty and unvarying aim shall be,
To make its millions happy, wise, and free.

XV.

Of those with whom thou sufferedst here and bled,
Our country's, Freedom's, little gallant band!
The larger portion mingle with the dead,
While near their graves the living remnant stand:
All, all, those chieftains whose embattled breasts,
With thine, stood firm in war's terrific van,
Have laid in dust their bright—their conquering crests;
E'en he, the Chief of Chiefs, that god-like man—
Our Washington! now sleeps in Vernon's tomb—
But Glory's beams their laurelled graves illume!

XVI.

Those council-sages, too, whose wisdom shone,
As Heaven's high radiance, pure and bright;
Whose thunders from our senates jarred the throne
Of England's king, and tyrants shook with fright;
All with their slumbering fathers now repose,
Save, scattered here and there, a lingering few,
Whose honoured heads are wreathed with gathered snows,
Whose hearts now breathe to thee a last adieu!
Once more on earth by thy loved presence blessed,
They feel prepared for their eternal rest.—

XVII.

The places where those sleeping patriots dwelt,
Their children, and their children's offspring, fill;
These bow at shrines round which their fathers knelt,
And where their fathers bled, their blood would spill.
When we impassioned benedictions breathe
Upon the memories of our martyred sires,
Fresh garlands round their trophied statues wreathe,
And o'er their urns relume the votive fires;
Thy consecrated name, conjoined with theirs,
Our gratitude—our deep devotion shares.—

XVIII.

"That here a nation's love embalms thy fame,
And millions thy exalted worth revere,
Behold evinced in their recorded claim (2)
To invite their generous benefactor here!
A grateful, young, enthusiastic race,
On Freedom's rich enjoyments fed,
All yearned to gaze upon the reverend face
Of him whose youthful blood for them was shed;
Whose lofty virtues brought him from afar,
To triumph, or to die, in Freedom's war.

XIX.

"To thee, in their imploring country's name,
By one to Liberty and thee endeared, (3)
Who had for her withstood the battle's flame,
And by his deeds her fainting votaries cheered—
Whence he the nation's highest honours wore—
This people's chartered wishes were conveyed.
Affection's guileless seal the message bore,
And on thy heart the expected impress made;
For soon, in kind accord with its request,
Thy head was pillowed on Columbia's breast.—

XX.

" Thy presence filled the exulting land with joy,
  Through all its peopled regions rapture ran;
To every tongue thy praises gave employ—
  The nation shouted—'Hail, thou matchless man!'
Scar-honoured veterans, worn and bowed with age,
  Partakers of thy sufferings and thy toil,
Who had with thee once trod th' ensanguined stage,
  And shared with thee in victory's glorious spoil,
Went forth to meet their brother and their friend—
And with his own their tears and transports blend.

XXI.

" The youthful sons and daughters of the land
  To whom thy honoured person was unknown,
Felt their warm hearts with ecstacy expand,
  Whilst in their eyes sublimest feelings shone—
As they the rapture-kindling tidings learned
  That thou wert on their country's happy shores
While that for which their bosoms long had burned—
  To spread their gratitude's exhaustless stores
Before the noblest champion of mankind—
Was now the joyful task to them assigned.—

XXII.

A Father's greeting—when from journeying long
In foreign climes, through perils dark and dire,
He meets again the dear domestic throng
Who spread the feast, and tune the rapturous lyre;—
With smiles and open arms around him press,
With melting looks gaze on his altered form,
And gladden him with many a fond caress;
A Father's greeting thus sincere and warm—
Thus flowing unconstrained from hearts benign—
My country's, Freedom's reverend friend! was thine.

XXIII.

Not thine the fleeting triumph of an hour,
It filled the compass of the rolling year!
Throughout the land, in hall and festive bower,
Where solemn fanes their sounding arches rear.
Where pleasure and the jocund dance obtain,
And wit, and song, and gayety preside;
From farthest mountain height to lowland plain,
In cities vast, where rolls the living tide,
And through the scattered peasants' rural grounds,
Thy triumph's gratulating strain resounds.

XXIV.

"Not thine the oppressive conqueror's withering march,
  Whose gore-stained chariot drags his loitering show;
For thee the hands of Freemen raise the laurelled arch,
  And o'er thy path their flowery offerings strow:
The voice that on our shores thy landing hailed,
  Through all the circle of thy wide career,
In liveliest notes of deepening joy, prevailed,—
  A nation's voice spontaneous and sincere!
Whose pealing transports in their vast embrace,
Comprise the present, past, and future race!

XXV.

"Too soon, alas! the light thy presence sheds
  Will cease to pour its cheering splendours here,
For, lo! this gathering crowd that round us spreads
  Proclaims, loved Chief! our parting moment near;
That, drawn by strong affection's kindred ties,
  Thou soon again wilt brave the billowy deep,
Returning hence to where thy native skies
  O'erarch the graves in which thy fathers sleep,
And bend their fragrant canopy around
The scenes to which thy tenderest hopes are bound.

XXVI.

"To Him whose voice the winds and seas obey,
The hearts of millions will in prayers arise,
That He may bless thy journey's dangerous way
With prospering breezes and propitious skies;
And yield thee back to thy beloved La Grange
Affection's dearest transports there to find:
That, happy in the sweetest interchange
Of kindred feeling, and congenial mind,
Thou freely mayest partake enjoyments there
Intense as those thy visit kindled here.

XXVII.

"Go, then, since thus unyielding Fates decree—
Return to Gallia's rich and blooming clime—
The land of genius and of chivalry!
Renowned for generous thought and deeds sublime;
Adorned by many a high and princely name,
In whose resplendent and illustrious line,
None ranks more nobly on the rolls of fame
Columbia's, Freedom's friend! than thine.
Along the dusky track of ages past
Its trophied monuments their radiance cast.

XXVIII.

"Thy honours, burnished into brighter glow,
Henceforth her proudest annals shall illume;
And should a stranger e'er desire to know
What name around her twines the fairest bloom,
And call upon a son of France to say
Who best among her worthies of his age,
Doth in *his* own *her* character display;
He'll point to thy bright name on glory's page,
While patriot blood shall mantle in his cheek,
And virtuous pride his beaming eye bespeak.

XXIX.

"And we, too, love to claim thee as our own—
Thou art to us and to our children bound
By ties whose strength, when centuries have flown,
Shall still in undiminished force be found.
As ours we claim thee by that matchless zeal
Whose more than patriot fire thy arm impelled
To wield in our behalf thy conquering steel,
When carnage here its gory orgies held,
And at the awful crisis of her doom
Our country was involved in darkest gloom.

XXX.

"And by that ligament of love which binds
In union stronger than the powers of death,
Freedom's exalted and congenial minds,
And braves uninjured Time's corrosive breath;
Which intertwines in ever-during fame
With that of our immortal Washington,
Thy brilliant, pure, and consecrated name,
Illustrious man! we claim thee as our own!—
By these—and all the soul's most holy ties—
We love thee with a love that never dies!

XXXI.

"Although with aching heart and trembling hands,
We take the bitter cup that fate extends,
And mourn that we must bow at those commands
Whose fiat severs Freedom's dearest friends;
Yet o'er that cup there shines a cheering beam,
And, mingled with its dark and chilling wave,
We taste delicious comfort's soothing stream,
Whose joyful influence shall our bosoms save
From hopeless grief—depression's gloomiest power—
E'en in the crisis of our parting hour!

XXXII.

"We know that in whatever clime thou art,
Loved Chief! our country and our country's weal
Will share the warm affections of thy heart,
Until that generous heart shall cease to feel;
And we the enrapturing hope indulge, kind friend!
That here again our joyful souls with thine,
On Freedom's themes, in converse sweet shall blend,
While tranquil here thy evening glories shine,
Diffusing round Columbia's hemisphere,
Their radiant light through many a happy year.

XXXIII.

"And now, the organ of my country's will,
But wanting powers of language to impart
The feelings that her myriad bosoms thrill—
As though they centred in one mighty heart—
Their love so ardent, uniform, and true,
So deep their sorrow, on this painful day;
I bid thee, in my country's name, adieu!—
With feelings that our tears can best convey—
That silent eloquence alone can tell—
I tender thee a nation's fond farewell!"

THE VALEDICTORY.

CANTO II.

I.

HERE, in reply, the reverend Chieftain rose,
And uttered thus the emotions of his breast :—
" 'Mid all the kindness that around me flows—
The blessings I enjoy as Freedom's guest—
And tokens of a nation's generous love,
To me, through you, her civic Chieftain, shown;
Most ardently my bosom glows to prove
The gratitude its deep sensations own;
And, for this fair occasion kindly given
To speak its feelings, breathes its thanks to Heaven.

II.

"To have, in their precarious, tender age,
Been cherished and adopted by these STATES
As their own Son, and when the deadly rage
That on the march of furious War awaits,
Around them poured its desolating ire;
To have, beneath their hallowed banners, stood.
And toiled to guard the spark of Freedom's fire—
Which tyrants aimed to quench in patriot blood;
Of all my thoughts embalmed in memory's shrine,
These are, to me, among the most divine!

III.

"Thus, in the cause of Liberty and Right,
Your fathers' deathless honours to have shared;
With them, when Freedom's temple crowned with light,
In this fair land by gallant hands was reared,
To have partaken in their glorious toil,
And, while the splendour of her towering fane
Makes distant tyrants from her powers recoil,
And threatens to subdue their iron reign,
To feel myself the joy her smiles impart,
Pours tides of transport through my swelling heart.

IV.

"To view the high exemplar founded here
Of SOCIAL ORDER spreading wide its power,
And Error's mouldering fabrics disappear
From realms where centuries gone had seen them lower;
While honoured for the humble aid I'd given
To bring around that happy change of things
By which despotic manacles were riven,
And guilt exposed that from oppression springs;
Have formed, in scenes of darkness and of strife,
My comfort through a long eventful life.

V.

"But where can I such glowing language find
As would in their appropriate tints portray,
The welcomes here, affectionate and kind,
The splendid and magnificent display,
And all the proofs that generous hearts can show
Of boundless kindness and attachment strong,
That poured around me in continuous flow,
'Mid rural scenes, and in the city's throng,
Through each bright moment of the glorious year
Which closed my recent journey's proud career?

VI.

"How shall my soul her grateful feelings own
To all the millions of this prosperous land,
For countless honours thus benignly shown?
What vivid force of words can I command
To paint the ardent thanks that swell my breast,
For favours high—munificence supreme—
By which Columbia's councils have expressed,
Towards me, intense affection and esteem,
While this whole people, with approving voice,
At these distinguished kindnesses rejoice?

VII.

"But pleasures more enrapturing still were mine!
Wherever my delightful journey led
The most exuberant proofs of power divine
Around me their sublime enchantments spread;
And Culture, guided by enlightened Art,
To Nature's rich magnific beauties gave
That fruitful influence which its smiles impart,
Where Science shines, and Freedom's banners wave:
The wilderness had changed to fields of bloom,
And light supplied the place of vanished gloom.

VIII.

"Unrivalled happiness on every hand,
Dependant on the people's sovereign will;
Prosperity o'erspreading all the land—
Unnumbered breasts prepared their blood to spill,
Ere tyrants hence should wrest a single right;
Harmonious order in the social plan—
Good sense, and all the virtues that unite
To dignify the character of man,
And guide him safely o'er life's stormy tide—
My eye entranced, my bosom thrilled with pride.

IX.

"In these transcendent blessings I surveyed
The grand results of principles sublime,
For which the patriot here unsheathed his blade,
And fought, and toiled, in danger's darkest time;
Of principles whose hallowed charter came
From God's own hand, when he on man impressed
His sacred image, and infused the flame
Of quenchless life through his exalted breast;
Which guard with equal care the poor man's right;
And his whose name is clothed with splendid might.

X.

"And in these blessings proudly I behold
Exemplified, with most conclusive force,
With all the power existing facts unfold—
And lights that stream from Truth's refulgent source—
The high pre-eminence which Freedom bears,
In all that's virtuous, beautiful, and great,
O'er aught that dire Oppression's impress wears,
Whate'er the name in which it grinds a state—
In which it stamps its ignominious brand,
Upon a prostrate and degraded land.—

XI.

"The base on which these cheering prospects rest—
On which this vast Republic stands secure—
Though tempests may her fortresses molest,
And siren blandishments her sons allure,
Is UNION OF THESE STATES. This is the rock
Whose giant power can every danger brave,
And crush its foes in their own reckless shock
Until their race is whelmed in Ruin's grave.
To guard this Union, then, with vestal zeal,
Behooves the friends of truth and human weal.

XII.

"To cherish it with never slumbering care—
And its assailants spurn as Freedom's foes—
To us—was our great Father's farewell prayer;
And when the dying patriot's life-blood flows
On fields where hosts for Liberty expire;
Or, when on beds of peaceful down he lies—
That latest times may find it still entire,
He pleads, in his last supplicating sighs;
While fettered regions, in this Union, see
The pledge of hopes that they shall yet be free!

XIII.

"But how, my loved and valued friend! shall I
Evince the grateful sentiments I feel,
For your avowed regards and favours high,
Displayed with all a brother's glowing zeal—
Your kind allusions to those hallowed days,
And brethren, whose remembrance melts my soul!
To my eventful journey's checkered ways
Since first my eye was fixed on Freedom's goal;
And for your thrilling glance at those delights
Which, in this land, have crowned my days and nights?

XIV.

"And where in all her rich and brilliant stores,
Can eloquence such bright expressions yield—
Or fancy, that on seraph pinions soars,
Such colours find in her ethereal field,
As can the feelings paint that warm my heart,
Enkindled by your strong pathetic view
Of this afflicting hour, when I must part
From scenes endeared, and bid these shores adieu—
That from your tender references spring
And sheathe the point of sorrow's sting?

XV.

"Of these, none more commanding claims advance
To my regards, than that which kindly turned
On climes most dear to me—my native France!
Where still the fires of Freedom are inurned—
Where deep and liveliest sympathies abound
With all the fortunes of this prosperous land,
And numerous brave and patriot breasts are found
Prepared the march of despots to withstand;
To form a bulwark round Truth's sacred shrine
And in her cause their gallant lives resign.

XVI.

"Deep, deep the impression in my bosom made
By your remarks, so touchingly addressed
To hopes that death—death only can invade—
To hopes, the dearest solace of my breast,
That I once more your country shall behold.
O! here, where honoured as a favoured son,
I've long among her veterans been enrolled,
May I, beside our Father Washington,
When all my toils and earthly duties close,
Lay down this wearied body to repose!

XVII.

"Suffice it now my feelings to declare,
As best in this sad hour I briefly may,
That, were my heart to your inspection bare,
The glowing sentiments it would display
Concurrent with the effusions from it poured
Throughout my recent glorious jubilee,
To these a solemn sanction would afford;
For these, in all their strength and fervency.
'Twill be my pride, my joy, to ratify,
Until my bosom heaves its latest sigh.

XVIII.

"On you, in whom, e'en from your boyhood's hour,
I've found a kind and meritorious friend,
May Heaven its choicest benedictions shower!
And on this Nation may its smiles descend!
That she may grow in grandeur and in might,
And happiness through all her borders reign—
That virtue here, and wisdom, may unite
To consecrate her beautiful domain,
And bless her with the Almighty's holy care,
Shall be my constant and my dying prayer!"

XIX.

Here closed our veteran Guest's sublime reply,
And through the crowd the deep contagion ran
Which told the solemn moment now was nigh,
When they must part from that exalted man:
The heart-born tear rolls down his reverend face,
And his majestic bosom heaves with grief
While he enfolds in his revered embrace—
His sorrowing friend—Columbia's honoured chief—
And once again, ere yet he leaves these shores,
For us God's blessings fervently implores.—

XX.

Those martial ranks—that music's plaintive strains—
Yon grave procession's melancholy march—
Those silent thousands covering hills and plains—
And solemn peals that shake the ethereal arch—
The Hero's deeply-mourned departure tell—
To him the Nation's parting homage pay:
And, lo! to her he bows a long farewell,
And down Potomac's tide is borne away!
While o'er her Capitol, with lingering eye,
And throbbing breast, he views her banners fly.

XXI.

But honours still the chieftain's course attend—
Along yon wharves behold the mingling crouds—
See where those closely peopled masts ascend—
Behold those clustered decks and spars and shrouds!
Her population there—her aged and young—
Both sons and daughters—Alexandria pours;
There, breathed from many a flowing heart and tongue,
In prayer to Heaven, her farewell incense soars—
In prayers that blessings, deathless and divine,
May round his heart their balmy wreaths entwine.

XXII.

Lo! yonder groups of free-born peasantry—
Who, e'en in childhood, learned the names to bless
Of those who bled to make their country free—
Along Potomac's honoured stream they press,
To yield the tribute of their guileless hearts
To Gallia's chief, ere from Columbia's shore,
Upon the deep, his reverend form departs:
And they, too, Heaven's protecting powers implore,
To guard him safely o'er the dangerous main,
And waft him to his native France again.

XXIII.

Now, silent on the deck the Hero stands!
An awful paleness wraps his mournful face;
Upon his breast he folds his trembling hands,
While grief marks on his brow her saddest trace.
How pores his eye, in tenderest agony,
Where yonder verdant height o'erlooks the wave!
That spot, enshrined in holiest sanctity,
Is Freedom's altar—Vernon's hallowed grave!
There on his memory solemn visions rise—
And vanished scenes endeared by Friendship's ties.

XXIV.

That form, serene, majestic, and sublime,
Which oft in all its glory he 'd beheld,
When battle-tempests darkened Freedom's clime,
Triumphing where their direst vengeance swelled;
That form which often, too, in peaceful guise,
'Mid Vernon's shades in happier days he 'd seen,
Before his thrilling Fancy seems to rise,
And there, with radiant and supernal mien,
Himself, in well-remembered tones, to greet,
And, pointing Heaven-ward, breathe, "We there shall meet!"

XXV.

Now evening spreads her dusky mantle round,
And shrouds the scene in sympathetic gloom;
A deeper grandeur clothes the sacred ground
Where angels hover near yon honoured tomb.
Still there the Hero's aching eye is cast
Till gathering darkness dims the mournful view:—
But now his lingering farewell gaze is past,
That sigh proclaims his heart's profound adieu!
While sorrow felt by none but loftiest souls,
In silence through his reverend bosom rolls.

XXVI.

The billow-cleaving engine plies its power—
Mount Vernon's consecrated grave recedes;
Night's gloomiest spirits rule the solemn hour—
Ascend her car, and loose her sable steeds;
Hark! floating from those melancholy clouds, (4)
Is heard their plaintive and condoling wail!
The pall of grief all heaven and earth enshrouds—
Potomac murmurs on the sweeping gale
As though her heaving, dark, and troubled waves,
To mourn with him, had left their liquid caves.—

XXVII.

Profound abstraction wraps the Hero's mind,
And on that tomb revered his thoughts converge;
While on his couch in solitude reclined,
His head is pillowed o'er the bounding surge.
In visions solemn, glorious and sublime,
His bosom's painful glooms dissolve away—
His eye pervades the depths of future time,
And sees the world enjoying Freedom's sway;
While, in communion with her patriot dead,
He feels the happiness for which they bled.—

XXVIII.

Another morning dawns upon the world,
But not in bright and cheering pomp arrayed;
The sun, with cloudy mantle round him furled,
Dispenseth not his wonted light and shade:
A canopy monotonous and drear,
O'er sombre wave, and misty shore, extends;—
The daring seaman gazes round with fear
That danger in the murky vault impends—
While there the Hero's sad attendants see,
Their grief condoled in Nature's sympathy.

XXIX.

Still onward, through the dark and rolling tide,
The labouring wheels impel the rapid boat:
As borne upon the air in buoyant pride—
Where vast and deep the billowy tempests float—
The daring eagle holds his arduous flight,
And sweeps along the bosom of the storm
Unawed by thunders, whirlwinds, and by night;
So, her distinguished voyage to perform,
That bark the elemental danger braves,
And rides adventurous o'er the lofty waves.

XXX.

Behold! half buried in the distant clouds,
Those stately masts like towering palm-trees rise!
While, there, wide-streaming o'er that vessel's shrouds!
Columbia's flag in pride and glory flies!
How dear to Freedom are its glittering stars!
What hopes will flutter in those snow-white sails—
Now stretched like sheeted giants on yon spars—
When they expand to catch the Ocean gales!
When, o'er the liquid mountains of the main,
They waft the Gallic Hero home again!

XXXI.

Her goal in view—those emblem stars her guide—
The Vernon thither points her dauntless beak;
With swifter might her pinions beat the tide,
And wondering sounds her ecstacy bespeak!
Well may his heart with patriot transports glow,
Who in that gallant ship an interest owns;
And as he sees her buoyant streamers flow,
His feelings pour in deep admiring tones;—
For she from chaos rose at Art's command, (5)
Like some proud fabric reared by Fancy's wand.—

XXXII.

Behold her strong-built battlements ascend!
While her proud bearing swells upon the sight;
No more with clouds her warlike features blend,
But stand forth all distinct in deepening light:—
At distance, thus, at first obscurely seen,
Some princely castle meets the approaching eye;
And circling mists enfold its stately mien,
Until, at length, the admiring gaze draws nigh—
When its vast towers emerge in prospect clear,
And all its parts in all its strength appear.

XXXIII.

Beneath those bulwarks now the Vernon glides—
And moored amidst that buoyant little fleet, (6)
Securely on the rocking billow rides—
While glowing breasts her joyful presence greet.
To hail the illustrious Chief with honours due,
That peerless ship unfolds her best array,
Spreads forth among her shrouds her gallant crew,
And bids them Freedom's noblest guards display!
Columbia's self-enrolled, unconquerable tars,
With laurelled brows, and bosoms trenched with scars.

XXXIV.

The Vernon now her honoured charge resigns—
On her his parting benedictions rest—
The cannon's peal with martial strain combines,
To welcome to that ship her reverend guest.
The swift-oared barge, and ornamental car, (7)
Have borne him o'er the intervening space—
He treads that ample deck unstained by war—
With deep emotions mingling in his face!
With thoughts that range the last eventful age
O'er deeds that yet shall grace the epic page!

XXXV.

In free and solemn interchange of soul,
With his attendant band of circling friends,
The Hero's few remaining moments roll—
Ere he to them the parting hand extends!—
That anxious, fleeting interval is gone—
And breasts are strained to his in farewell clasp—
Loved forms he ne'er again may look upon—
Worn down by giant Time's unwearied rasp:—
And youthful patriots—sons of veteran sires—
His prayers receive—and glow with purer fires!

XXXVI.

That painful valedictory now is o'er!
The winged boats their homeward journey urge—
While many a heart, with heavy anguish sore,
Is borne reluctant o'er the foaming surge;
And eyes, still eager for another gaze
Upon the form of that receding Chief,
Are poring through the half-impervious haze
Until their failing vision's drowned in grief,
And Friendship's left to employ its grateful zeal
In aspirations for his future weal.—

XXXVII.

Like some proud courser bearing on the rein,
And vaulting high, impatient of delay,
That stately ship doth on her moorings strain,
In haste to bound along the watery way;—
But doomed awhile to wait the favouring breeze,
She towers alone in stationary pride—
While from her sides recoil the broken seas,
And back like vanquished hosts in battle glide;
While her stern tars the veering clouds explore,
And hear with hope the billow's lessening roar.

XXXVIII.

Must she, with boding glooms around her cast,
Spread forth her virgin canvass on the deep?
Will not kind Heaven arrest the lowering blast—
Disperse the rack—and bid the tempests sleep?
'Tis done! celestial splendour bursts around!
Auspicious smiles invest the unfolding skies—
While, from their bright and gorgeous western bound,
The sun pours on soft clouds his golden dies,
Along the waves his glittering mantle spreads,
And joy through many an anxious bosom sheds.

XXXIX.

While garlands, culled from Glory's richest bowers,
The honoured Chieftain's hoary brows entwine,
And Freedom, clothed in her sublimest powers,
Inscribes his name where deathless tablets shine;
Still more distinguished honours round him beam!
A higher auspice rules and guards his weal—
See, o'er him curved, that Rainbow's vivid stream! (8)
Whose tints such pure ethereal charms reveal—
Shall Faith's strong ken not there, unblamed, descry
A halo formed for him by hands on high?

XL.

In that bright token of superual love,
  Well may Lafayette's friends their hopes repose—
Assured that he shall find an arm above,
  In danger's hour, to shield his breast from woes.—
Thy canvass, then, majestic ship! expand,
  And bear away before that favouring gale;
Soon shalt thou reach the Hero's blooming land,
  Where joyful bosoms shall thy presence hail;
While his loved offspring, from her fragrant shore,
Shall blessings on thy name, and Freedom's, pour.

XLI.

Of Ocean's ample fleet thenceforth the pride,
  Thou shalt, through many an age of after time,
O'er distant seas, in radiant glory, ride,
  And wave thy flag inscribed with deeds sublime.
And should'st thou e'er a foe in battle join,
  That flag's untarnished stars—thy country's fame—
That unforgotten symbol's rays divine—
  And, leagued with these, thy never-dying name,
Shall arm thy guardian band with quenchless fire,
And bid them triumph, or in blood expire!—

NOTES

TO

THE VALEDICTORY.

NOTE (1).

Potomac's kindred cities, &c.

Washington, Alexandria, Georgetown.

NOTE (2).

Behold evinced in their recorded claim, &c.

Referring to a unanimous Resolution of Congress, requesting the President of the United States to invite General Lafayette to visit this country, &c.

NOTE (3).

By one to liberty and thee endeared.—

James Monroe.

NOTE (4).

Hark! floating from those melancholy clouds.

A storm, accompanied by rain, set in early in the evening, and continued until late on the succeeding day.

NOTE (5).

For she from Chaos rose at Art's command,

Like some proud fabric reared by Fancy's wand.—

The Brandywine was completely equipped for her voyage in two months after she was launched!

NOTE (6).

And moored amidst that buoyant little fleet.

Besides her own boats, there were at this time lying near the Frigate, the steam-boats, Constitution of Baltimore, and Surprize, of Georgetown.

NOTE (7).

———— *and ornamented car.*

General Lafayette was elevated to the deck of the Brandywine in a splendid chair, prepared by Captain Morris for the occasion, and supported on decorated cordage.

See a well-written and interesting "Account of a Trip to the Brandywine, by one of the Gentlemen who accompanied General Lafayette, in a Letter addressed to the Editor of the National Journal."

NOTE (8).

See, o'er him curved, that Rainbow's vivid stream!

The storm having dispersed, a beautiful Rainbow appeared, encircling the Brandywine, with its centre directly over her. See the letter referred to in the foregoing note.

ODES.

LAFAYETTE'S DEPARTURE.

AN ODE.

I.

BEHOLD Columbia weeping stand
Upon her shore, with anguish dumb!
The pall of grief enshrouds the land,
And hushed is labour's cheering hum:
Her dearest Friend is from her bosom torn,
And, lo! by fate to foreign climes is borne.—

II.

When on her breast exposed and bare,
Oppression's storm with vengeance beat,
His wealth and blood he scorned to spare,
'Till he beheld her foes retreat:
And then, for her, with all a patriot's zeal
Was still prepared to draw his generous steel.—

III.

A friend so gallant, kind, and true,
Might well Columbia's heart have won ;—
She loves him with devotion due,
Her Benefactor and her Son !*
A pilgrim to her arms in age he came,
But leaves her now, recalled by duty's claim.—

IV.

How swells his breast--how streams his eye—
As here he casts his parting view
On fields o'erarched by Freedom's sky,
And waves to them his sad adieu!
Like glowing incense wafted o'er the seas,
His solemn prayer for us is on the breeze!

V.

" Blessed home of Freedom! land endeared!
To thee my bosom fondly cleaves;
I still behold thy graves revered,
Where many a snow-white column heaves
mark the ground where patriot martyrs sleep,
oary pilgrims love to pause and weep.—

* By adoption.

VI.

"Dear hallowed ground! Oh sacred graves!
To you my soul with ardour clings;
Around the grass that o'er you waves,
May seraphs spread their guardian wings;
For underneath your verdant turf repose
The hearts of noblest men—Oppression's foes!

VII.

"Immortal band of gallant souls!
With whom in glorious fields I've stood,
When battle thunders shook the poles,
And earth's green robe was drenched in blood!
In fresh remembrance still my glowing heart
Will hold your worth—though from your tombs I part!—

VIII.

Elysian land of Liberty!
On thee may Heaven its blessings shed—
From age to age mayest thou be free—
By virtue loved—the tyrant's dread!
May fettered realms thy chartered glories read,
And learn from thee to conquer while they bleed!

IX.

"Loved land of beauty, and of power!
May thy example light the world,
Until revolves the glorious hour
When despots from their thrones are hurled!
And not a region on wide earth remains
Where Freedom has not reared her holy fanes.—

X.

"And is this fading view the last—
The last these aged eyes shall take
Of thee, dear land!—Oh now 'tis past!
And will this throbbing heart not break!
Sustain me Heaven! and grant that I once more
May tread in peace Columbia's happy shore!"—

XI.

Thus breathed the veteran's heaving breast,
While vanished in the distant blue
The shores his smiles—his prayers—had blessed,
And he from Vernon's tomb withdrew!
To leave that tomb, the patriots' holiest shrine,
Wrings blood from ties that round his heart-strings twine.

XII.

May angel bands the bark convoy
  That wafts the reverend Hero on—
And to La Grange, and all its joy,
  Restore him and his gallant son!
Long may thy evening beams, Lafayette, shine—
And gild the world with their serene decline!—

LAFAYETTE'S JUBILEE.

AN ODE.

I.

HE came—the gallant warrior came—
   Across the stormy flood
To where he 'd braved the battle-flame,
   And poured his youthful blood.
His body bore the marks of time,
   But still his soul was young!
His bosom glowed with thoughts sublime,
   And wisdom tuned his tongue.

II.

As spread before his joyful eyes
  The green and lovely shore,
Where he had seen war-tempests rise
  And heard their thundering roar;
As there, with peace and virtue blessed,
  He Freedom's sons beheld
Reposing on her fostering breast,
  His heart with transport swelled.—

III.

To view their country's reverend friend
  Rejoicing millions ran;
Where'er Columbia's bounds extend
  They hailed the godlike man:
Throughout his course from state to state,
  A stream of glory shone—
A triumph his supremely great,
  To conquering kings unknown!—

IV.

Not his the fame of deadly glare
  Whose fiery ray consumes;
But such as virtue loves to share—
  As gilds our fathers' tombs!
No slaves in chains before him bow,
  He dreads no tyrant's frown;
The wreath of Freedom binds his brow—
  He 'd scorn to wear a crown!—

V.

While, greeted with prolonged applause,
  He treads Columbia's shore,
No canker-worm of Conscience gnaws
  His bosom's guiltless core:—
Not his the oppressor's jubilee
  Where tongues are forced to laud;
Here happy hearts, sincere and free,
  His generous deeds applaud.—

VI.

The scenes he saw in visions high,
  When from his darling France
He hither turned his youthful eye,
  Now meet his raptured glance.
In all their actual grandeur here,
  And living charms arrayed—
Wherever shines his bright career—
  Those scenes are now displayed.

VII.

Where boundless forests spread their gloom,
  And tawny Indians roamed,
He sees a land of culture bloom;
  And, where the wild wave foamed
Around the native's beechen skiff,
  Beholds the white-winged sail,
Swift as the eagle from his cliff,
  Borne on the mountain gale.—

VIII.

Here, towering in its daring might,
He views the free-born mind,
And sees a nation gathering light
From sources unconfined!
Around him here majestic rise,
On nature's sacred plan,
Those fabrics, beautiful and wise,
That guard the rights of man.—

IX.

Thy joys, Lafayette, how divine!
As here, on Freedom's soil
Adorned—enriched—by deeds of thine—
By thy own blood and toil—
Thou see'st its fruits luxuriant rise,
And round the cottage bloom,
While far beyond Columbia's skies
They cast their sweet perfume.

THE BIRTHDAY OF LAFAYETTE.

AN ODE.

I.

AROUND the golden portals of the morn,
In shining bands celestial minstrels play;
Their strains proclaim a glorious Chief was born—
A patriot warrior—on this honoured day.
From orb to orb the kindling rapture flies,
And sweeps the vast orchestra of the skies.

II.

Exulting earth the joyful era hails,
A brighter lustre kindles o'er her hills,
A deeper verdure clothes her sparkling vales,
And sweeter music through her woodlands thrills:
While regions wrapped in chains, and whelmed in night,
Are cheered on this glad morn with Hope's mild light.—

III.

Well may thy lovely lands rejoice, O Earth!
At this illustrious day's returning beams,
Since Heaven ordained for them the Hero's birth
Which ranks its fame with Freedom's loftiest themes;
Since for those lands his arm was clothed with power,
His soul inspired to rule in danger's hour.—

IV.

But where, O where, in all the choral joy
That swells the transports of this day sublime,
Can praises more sincere the heart employ
Than burst from glowing breasts in Freedom's clime?
For here that arm, that soul, through flames and blood,
Through storms and death, repelled Oppression's flood.

V.

While yet the bloom of boyhood flushed his cheek,
And courtly honours clustered round his brow;
His heart, in valour firm, in virtue meek,
At Freedom's shrine preferred his gallant vow:
High o'er Ambition's aim his spirit rose,
And scorned the fame that feeds on human woes.

VI.

His view she pointed from her cloudless height
To where our fathers on the ravaged field
Were battling with the pride of England's might,
And many a noble eye in death was sealed:
As there he saw the crimson tempest roll,
Celestial visions flashed upon his soul!

VII.

A world for human happiness designed,
He through the battle whirlwind there beheld;
No more the arms of love that round him twined,
Nor patriot passion that his bosom swelled,
In Gallia's precincts could his soul restrain;
He broke from love—from France—and crossed the main.

VIII.

Here long he toiled with Freedom's chosen band,
Here deeds of glorious splendour crowned his fame;
His generous blood was shed to save our land,
And beauty blessed, and infants lisped his name:
His bounty hushed the orphan's mournful cry,
And soothed the pang that barbed misfortune's sigh.

IX.

Columbia, then, may well his birth-day hail
With tuneful harp, with pomp and song,
While sons from fathers learn the joyful tale
That shall from age to age his deeds prolong:
His fame, still brightening with the sweep of Time
While earth revolves, shall shine through every clime.

X.

What though upon his dear-loved native France
The trace of tyrant footsteps still is seen;
And there censorial courts with withering glance,
O'er struggling genius rear their gorgon mien:
There yet the truths by her great patriot taught,
Shall melt the chains that bind the wing of thought!

XI.

The time, erelong, shall come, when Freedom's voice
O'er Gallia's fragrant vine-wreathed hills shall rise,
On this her *people's* proudest day rejoice,
And pour thanksgivings through her radiant skies:
Then, then, Lafayette! shall thy glory stand
The loftiest monument in all her land.

XII.

To thee a still uncancelled debt she owes,
Thy life was staked—thy wealth—thy peace—resigned,
To check the bloody torrent of her woes,
When Fury, armed with flames, enraged and blind,
Destruction through her blooming vineyards spread,
And yelled as Virtue from its vengeance fled.—

XIII.

When Murder, roaming through the midnight gloom,
In many a noble heart her dagger laved,
And heros on the scaffold found their doom,
Thy valiant breast the frantic horrors braved:
A pillar of sublime and splendid light,
Thy virtues towered through the awful night.

XIV.

Terrific demons ruled the stormy hour,
And Chaos brooded o'er the ruined land;
While dastard spirits trembled at thy power,
And bade it fall beneath the assassin's hand:
But shielded by the Almighty's holy arm,
Thy gallant life escaped th' impending harm.

XV.

Still on thy footsteps pressed, with blood-hound rage,
Thy ruthless foes—and still thy life was spared!—
Thy wrongs, enrolled on History's faithful page,
Shall fire the soul when patriot arms are bared
Where man, worn down by bonds, on Heaven shall call,
And rise in strength to burst his iron thrall.

XVI.

Then, from thy dungeons, Olmutz! sounds shall break,
Whose thunders, thrilling like some martial blast,
Shall fettered nations from long slumbers wake,
Hurl thrones to dust, and strike proud kings aghast!
And, then, in their own prisons' vaulted glooms,
Shall vanquished tyrants find congenial tombs.—

XVII.

Thy glory, reverend Chieftain! despots dread
In every realm that bows beneath their sway;
Where'er the fragrance of thy fame is shed,
Kind hope still casts on man her soothing ray;
And when the world no longer bears a throne,
Enfranchised millions shall thy virtues own.—

XVIII.

Let Freedom, then, her glittering banner rear,
And on her mountain heights let bonfires burn,
To hail thy natal day, from year to year,
While minstrel songs proclaim its glad return,
And beauty's voice, and childhood's artless tongue,
The chorus join, 'till through the world 'tis rung.

LINES,

Written after the Departure of Lafayette.

I.

COLUMBIA'S jubilee is o'er,
Her floods of joy subside;
Her friend—Lafayette—leaves her shore,
O'erwhelmed in sorrow's tide,
Farewell, Columbia's friend, farewell!
The gales that waft thee on,
The sighs of weeping millions swell,
Who mourn that thou art gone.

II.

Here late the blaze of welcome burned,
  And song and pomp proclaimed,
That Freedom's champion had returned
  To where his sword once flamed,
When struggling in the field of blood
  Against a haughty foe,
Her Spartan phalanx nobly stood,
  Returning blow for blow.

III.

But silence, now, and mournful gloom,
  Throughout the nation spread;
For here no more his smiles illume
  The land for which he bled.
His presence breathed a holy spell,
  That round our vast domain,
Like heavenly dews, or manna, fell,
  And vanquished care and pain.

IV.

Now that enrapturing spell has flown,
And care and pain return—
Hark! mingling with Columbia's moan,
Sounds burst from Freedom's urn—
" Farewell, my honor'd Son!"
In plaintive tones resound,
Where heaves the tomb of Washington
On Vernon's hallowed ground.

V.

Behold! the nation bows in prayer
For her departed guest:—
" Thy arm, Almighty Father, bare—
Send forth thy high behest,
To guard Columbia's reverend friend
From Danger's varied power;
May peace and joy his life attend,
And bless his final hour!"

THE BOW AND SMILE.

Lines Addressed to General Lafayette by a Little Girl, at whose Request they were written.

GREAT Chief! ere yet five annual suns had shed
Their radiant beams around my infant head,
I heard thy virtues pealed in notes of fame,
And learned to love and venerate thy name.

When told that I thy reverend face should view,
I felt the gush of joy my cheeks bedew;
And when the cannon's voice and rolling drum
Proclaim'd that thou, the great, the good, hadst come,
My little heart with glad emotions beat,
And rapture bore me through the thronging street,
Until my eyes thy glorious form beheld,
Where shouts of greeting thousands round thee swell'd.

One look of kindness, then, one smile from thee,
Were worth a thousand splendid toys to me;
But how could I, the humblest being there,
Such favour claim—such mark'd attention share?
Distinguished men, and beauty, round thee press'd,
Thy notice gain'd—by thy regards were bless'd:—
There martial bands in glittering armour shone,
And music breath'd in many a thrilling tone:
How then could I e'en hope, on that proud day,
Amid its joys sublime, and grand array,
That thy exalted thoughts, and glance benign,
Should rest one moment on a form like mine?
But still, towards thee, my eyes, my steps were turn'd,
And for one smile from thee my bosom burn'd,
When, pausing in thy transit through the crowd,
Thy eye met mine—to me thy head was bow'd!
And from thy noble features, free from guile,
Upon me beam'd thy gentlest, tenderest, smile!
Still, through my heart, I feel its melting glow,
And still it makes my tears of transport flow.

That bow, that smile, whate'er the unknown fate
That may my pilgrimage through life await,

Still treasured with my memory's richest gems,
I'll dearer hold than queens their diadems.

Those cherish'd tokens of thy kindness tell,
How mildest virtue can with greatness dwell;
How, free from proud Ambition's dazzling glare,
The loftiest Chief, with condescending care,
Can mark the movements of a humble child,
Nor deem his glory of one ray despoil'd:
How e'en amid the pomp, and gorgeous blaze,
That speak his fame, and blind the common gaze,
His zeal—his kind, his anxious zeal—is shown,
To make each bosom happy as his own.

For thee, my country's friend! my prayers shall rise,
When, borne away from Freedom's sheltering skies,
Thou art upon the raging ocean cast,
Exposed to yawning gulf and whelming blast;
And when, again, thou breath'st thy native clime,
Begirt by Freedom's foes, by chains, and crime,
O! may'st thou there in health and comfort find
Thy friends and all thy *loved ones* left behind!
And soon, with these, soon may'st thou hither come,
To plant in Freedom's soil thy final home!

And here may I, the gay, the happy child,
To whom the *good man* bow'd and smil'd,
Again his coming hail—his presence greet,
His smiles enjoy—his benedictions meet.

THE END.

Milton Keynes UK
Ingram Content Group UK Ltd.
UKHW040039281223
435071UK00008B/687

9 789354 540288